TAKE THREE BREATHS

A Short Course in Meditation and Mindfulness

M. A. Worthington-Hassall

A road in our walled compound in the UAE has a clump of trees at one corner where thousands of house sparrows gather come sunset. On a walk I stop and listen to them shouting, literally, imagining them jostling for the best positions in their tiny nests. The excitable chatter is comforting as it indicates to me that no matter what strife is going on in this world nature ignores it all, running its course regardless, as it has done for centuries.

Cheryl Robertson Mandy

Table of Contents

Cover: A possibly auspicious view of a rainbow taken from the grounds of the Buddhist Kadampa Temple for World Peace, which is situated on the coast near Ulverston, Cumbria in the English Lake District.

Copyright

ISBN-13: 978-1517237691
ISBN-10: 1517237696

Liability

The author shall have no liability to any person for loss or damage, however occurring, whether direct or indirect, resulting from the use of these course materials.

Medical Advice Disclaimer

If you require medical advice relating to a particular health problem, the author strongly recommends that you contact your doctor or medical practitioner. The author is not qualified to provide medical advice about health problems and nothing in the content of these course materials constitutes any form of medical advice. Any mindfulness or meditation techniques or information provided, should be regarded as complementary to, not a substitute for, conventional healthcare.

Dedication

To my wife Jeanette and my sons Benjamin and Joseph.

Special thanks to my editor Cheryl - also to Asher, Bill, Clare, Dawn, Delia, Helen, Janice, Kevin, MariaElena, Stephen and anyone who has attended the weekly meditation sessions here in Buckden, Cambridgeshire, England.

FOREWORD

The purpose of this short course is the elimination of fear or to put it another way – I want you to be happy. In this context I define happiness as a stable condition of inner wellbeing and contentment - a reservoir of support to guide you through life's many challenges. True happiness is like the stillness at the bottom of a warm, comforting, sea that remains unaffected by your daily problems, pleasures and pains that are the waves and ripples on its surface.

It is important to note that pleasure and joy are poor imitations of true happiness. Happiness cannot be achieved at the expense of others or from external activities. You are likely to find that most of the pleasure that you experience externally, is short-lived and quickly fades or can even change to dislike with repetition. Part of the human condition is that most of us live in state of suffering. Often we forsake happiness today for something that we think that we may want in the future or we don't notice what is happening now because we are dwelling on events that hurt us in the past. We frequently live with our mind elsewhere and this preoccupation means that we seldom notice the happiness of the present moment.

The problem is that searching for happiness externally is a fruitless journey that always leaves you wanting more. If you reflect on your achievements in your life so far you will likely find that the joy that each accomplishment gave you was short lived. Individuals who have achieved great success in their lives often find themselves living in the past, trying to relive old glories and ignoring the here and now. Conversely people who have been hurt earlier in their lives find it hard to be happy in the present because they carry the wounds of painful events that occurred in their past. Historical injury, whether real or imagined, festers in the mind and is repeated and amplified, causing yet more hurt to the unfortunate victim.

Meditation and mindfulness help us to live in the present and allow us to connect with our true selves. The practices described in this course are designed to make forgiveness possible and to take away fear. Without the fear that drives us to internal suffering, defence and attack we are, in essence, love. Once we have achieved a state, where we are able to truly love ourselves and be happy, we are then able to extend love to others. In simple terms, we become easy to be around and do not hurt others. We develop into teachers of love, peace, compassion and happiness simply by being. In this way we start to heal the wrongs, suffering, divisions and insanity of the world simply by being still and observing our thoughts.

This short course brings together a number of simple meditation and mindfulness exercises from many different cultures and customs. Included in the following pages are meditative practices that are based on meditations commonly used in Buddhism, Hinduism, Islam, Judaism, and Christianity along with other mindfulness techniques. In sharing these methods I aim to equip you with an array of ways of achieving a meditative state whilst also demonstrating the commonality rather than the diversity that is at the core of the world's spiritual traditions. I hope that you will enjoy performing this collection of practices and techniques so that you can learn some more about yourself and what really makes you happy.

My aim is to illustrate that the ability to meditate is part of being human and can be practiced by anyone irrespective of their way of life, background or religious persuasion.

This is a very exciting time in our human evolution because more of us are seeking inner peace and happiness. On one level it appears that we are becoming increasingly more material as the world becomes an ever larger global market place, but on another many more of us have access to information that was previously not available or shared with previous generations. The wonder of the internet makes it possible to download the majority of the holy texts, from the Koran to the Gnostic Gospels within a few minutes. Centuries of wisdom are available to you at the touch of a keypad and there are many paths to enlightenment that you can choose.

I ask you to start your journey by reading Chapter 1 and simply taking 'Three Breaths'. As you work through the exercises your true self will become your inner guide. All the theory in the world will not help you unless you put it into practice. The journey I want you to take is one of healing and you will not take the journey alone. Your path is not hard and you have access to all the help that you need – you have simply forgotten how to ask for it. I hope that this course will help you to remember how to love and how to be happy. It is not by accident that you read these words and I wish you well on your journey.

CHAPTER 1 – TAKE THREE BREATHS

Meditation has brought me much happiness and has helped me to eliminate the fear and anxiety that I experienced earlier in my life. Hopefully I can provide you with some of the knowledge and techniques that I have learnt during my practice and in turn you are able to pass them on to others you may meet along the way.

M. A. Worthington-Hassall

To start your journey through this short-course I simply ask you to take three breaths, but before you do, let me explain a little about how the breath is used in meditation. A large part of both meditation and mindfulness is about observing ourselves – our thoughts and our feelings. The breath is important in meditation because it is something that we all possess that happens right now – not in the past or in the future. We breathe without conscious thought – occasionally we notice changes in our breath, perhaps when we exercise heavily or struggle for breath due to an illness, but for the most part, it is something that we unconsciously let our body control automatically along with our heart-beat, digestive system and other bodily functions. The power and purity of observing the breath is fundamental to many meditation practices - let's start with the first exercise:

Sit down, with your feet flat on the floor, close your eyes and relax your body as much as you can. Gently take a deep breath in through your nose, keeping your mouth shut, so that you push your stomach area out rather than your chest so that you feel your tummy expanding

(like a big balloon!). Once your tummy is full of air continue to inhale so that your chest also

fills with air – fill your chest so full of air that you can feel it in your collar bone! As you finish

inhaling pause for a moment before slowly releasing your breath, taking approximately

twice as long to exhale as it took you to inhale, again through your nose.

As you take your second breath start to observe the cool air entering through your nostrils

as you inhale. Feel your stomach, followed by your chest, expanding as you draw your

breath in and become aware of any effect that it may have had on the rest of your body.

Again, pause at the, 'top of your breath', for a moment before gently and slowly releasing

the air from your body – as you do so notice the feel of the breath as it leaves your nose.

Repeat the exercise with your third breath, maintaining your focus, until you have inhaled

and exhaled once more. Once you have completed the exercise do not immediately open

your eyes – let your breathing fall back to its natural rhythm and then pause for a few

moments to reflect on how you now feel.

In the majority of cases the act of simply taking three breaths in the way that I describe will make you feel better and much calmer. By observing your breathing you have consciously built some space between what is sometimes called your, 'True Self', and your thoughts, emotions and feelings.

Many of us live our lives worrying about things that may or may not occur in the future or reliving events that hurt us in the past. This diminishes our ability to live in the present. We may miss things that are actually happening now, which is the only time that we really have to live our lives. People often suffer because they are afraid something from their past may hurt them in the future. Our minds spin with the many permutations of what the future may hold - either good or bad. Most of us seem to be willing to accept pain today because we dream that we can create a perfect tomorrow. Unfortunately, for most of us, the perfect tomorrow rarely arrives.

Doctors now tell us that stress increases the risk of disease, and when we are ill, stress reduces our chances of a speedy recovery. It therefore makes sense to reduce the stress in our lives. But how do we do this? There's always another problem that comes along to replace the last one.

To understand how we get stressed and how and why meditation can help let's take a look at the science behind meditation. Scientists studying our brainwaves have highlighted that there are patterns of brainwave activity that are associated with our day to day actions and behaviour. They have defined Alpha, Beta, Delta and Theta brainwave patterns in their studies that correspond to various frequencies of brainwave. These patterns are generally associated with activities such as wakefulness, meditative activity, light sleep and deep sleep. In this discussion I will focus primarily on describing Beta and Alpha states, however, for completeness, Theta patterns are associated with light sleep and delta brainwaves with deep sleep. Recent research has also identified gamma brainwaves, which are thought to be linked to bursts of insight, compassion and high-level information processing.

Beta brainwaves are commonly observed when we are awake. They are associated with the left side of the brain and they are strongly linked with a focus on what is happening around us including: planning, speculation, analysis, being busy, conscious thought and logical thinking. Beta brain patterns are rarely focused on the now and are generally associated with a focus that is outside of yourself. Having the right amount of Beta brainwaves allows us to complete tasks and work goals easily. Spending too much time in Beta can result in a person experiencing an inability to relax and can result in a person being subjected to excessive stress and/or anxiety in their lives.

In contrast to Beta, Alpha brain patterns are related to being rather than doing and are associated with the right side of the brain. When in Alpha we are feeling rather than thinking and are fully in the present without a focus on the past or future. Alpha waves help us to calm down, can promote feelings of deep relaxation and are linked with the gap between conscious thinking and the subconscious mind. Most people experience an Alpha state just before they go to sleep or just before they awake. You may find that you subconsciously scan your body prior to going to sleep and occasionally notice aches and pains in your body that you weren't aware of during your waking day. This is likely to be because you were distracted by the tasks that you were performing during the 'Beta' state of your working day. You may find (like most people) that you have conditioned yourself to expect sleep just after you have achieved an Alpha state, so when you are introduced to meditation, that induces an Alpha state, you may feel drowsy and may even fall asleep.

Alpha waves are reduced when our eyes are open or when we are feeling drowsy, which is why meditation is best performed with eyes closed and in a sitting position – lying down to meditate is likely to induce sleep and therefore, makes it less likely that an Alpha state be achieved. By using various meditation techniques we can move our mind into an Alpha state and this can help us to reduce the impact of stress in our lives. In addition meditation can remediate a phenomenon known as 'Alpha Blocking'. Alpha Blocking can occur in the brain when there is very little Alpha activity due to the dominance of Beta brain patterns. Often this occurs when we are over-stimulated and the Beta waves block the production of Alpha waves. The symptoms of this are that we find it hard to relax and can have difficulty in sleeping. A noteworthy benefit of learning to meditate is that it can help you to sleep better.

In truth we cannot really protect ourselves from the world, its problems and suffering, but we can change our attitude to it and the people around us. Whether you take a spiritual or scientific view of the universe, taking three breaths whenever you feel the smallest stress, fear or anxiety in your life is the start of your journey to happiness. Try to take three breaths when you are presented with situations where you are not in control e.g. traffic jams, train delays, long queues, flight cancellations, etc. Look at these moments, not as moments of anxiety or stress, but as opportunities for you to spend time with your inner self. In time you will come to understand that returning to your natural state of perfect inner happiness is a most important goal, both for you and those around you.

I hope that in performing the three breaths exercise that you found a moment of peace or relaxation that was enough for you to continue to explore the practice of meditation. Consciously taking three breaths regularly throughout your day, particularly in moments of stress, will greatly improve your wellbeing and change your life for the better. In the coming chapters I will explain why this is so and how mindfulness and meditation can transform your life. It is important to highlight that each individual chooses whether or not he or she is happy. In summary, happiness is your choice and you can choose to be happy right now!

NOTES...

CHAPTER 2 - BEING GRATEFUL

I learnt how to refocus on what is important in life and how not to stress about things that I cannot change. Also it is strange how you become more aware of your surroundings and the people within it. Some of the techniques have been invaluable e.g. learning to calm oneself down and clear the mind so you can sleep at night is brilliant. And the great thing is you can meditate anytime anywhere. Meditating for 10 minutes can make all the difference.

Carol-Anne Parish

Let's try a second exercise that you can use alongside the Three Breaths technique to move you forward in your meditational journey.

Please take a little longer with this exercise. Find a place where you are unlikely to be disturbed – somewhere you generally feel comfortable and secure. If you wish to use a meditation timer; set it for 15 or 20 minutes. You may also want to play some background music, choose something that you know will relax you – if you don't have any suitable music silence will work just as well. Observing the differences between performing the meditation with alternative pieces of music and then without any music may be something you wish to try, to see if it changes your meditation experience.

As with the previous exercise sit down on a chair with your feet flat on the floor, close your eyes, keep your back straight, cup your hands one on top of each other in your lap with your palms facing upwards and relax you body as much as you can... gently take a deep breath in through your nose, keeping your mouth shut, so that you push your stomach area out rather than inflating your chest (so that you feel your tummy expanding like a big balloon). As you finish inhaling pause for a moment before slowly releasing your breath, taking approximately twice as long for you to exhale as it took you to inhale, again through your nose. Follow the breath as you take three, four, five, six... breaths until you find that you fall into a natural rhythm of the breath coming in and the breath going out.

Keep the focus on your breathing as the minutes pass – you will notice your breaths becoming shallower as you relax into the meditation. Undoubtedly, thoughts will start to come into your mind and you will find that they will distract you from focussing on your breath. If this happens don't get annoyed with yourself, just gently return your focus back to your breathing and remember that the aim is to follow the breath and not your thoughts. An important misconception about meditation is that it requires you to make your mind become completely free of thoughts. This is absolutely not the case – the aim is for you to simply step back from your thoughts so that you don't involve yourself with them – you merely watch your thoughts go by and don't give them any energy by getting caught up with them.

The next stage of the meditation is to start to recognise things that you are grateful for. Inside your mind simply say thank you to yourself for each individual thing that you are grateful for. Do not try to distinguish between big and small or try to create any form of order – simply identify each individual item as it comes into your mind and say thank you for each one. You may be grateful for your children or your parents or perhaps the person who smiled, held the door for you and allowed you to pass through it before they did - it doesn't really matter, the important thing is that you are genuinely grateful.

In any meditative exercise don't try too hard. There is no right or wrong. In this case you may identify two or three things or twenty or thirty things to be grateful for, it's unique to each individual. When you feel that you have identified enough items simply return your focus back to your breathing. If you are using a timer wait until it sounds to tell you it's time to end your meditation – otherwise wait until you naturally feel that you should come back to a non-meditative state. It's important to come out of any meditation gently – take some deep breaths, wiggle hands and toes and take a few minutes to adjust before finally opening your eyes. You may wish to rub your face and body with your hands as a further act of completion – you may notice that your hands are warm when you do this.

Sometimes when you have completed a meditation you may feel a little lighted headed or even slightly intoxicated. This can be a very pleasant experience, but not that helpful if you need to drive a car or operate machinery after you have meditated. In such circumstances it is important to know how to, 'ground', yourself and this can be as simple as drinking some water or tea. I recommend that you prepare a glass or jug of water prior to meditation so that you can ground yourself by drinking a glass of water after you have meditated. In a group setting sharing a jug of water or a pot of mint tea can be an excellent way of 'grounding' everyone whilst also offering the social opportunity of sharing your experience of the meditation.

The practice of the above meditation is likely to change your attitude to your day-to-day life in subtle ways. You may take more pleasure from situations where people are nice to you, reciprocate more when someone helps you and become more aware of events that work in your favour. Becoming more mindful of such changes in your daily routine will be helpful to you.

NOTES...

CHAPTER 3 – A FOCUS ON RELAXATION

For the first time in over 50 years of my life I feel like I'm finally living.

Clare Fogden

Being mindful of our body is a good way of both relaxing and listening to what our body is trying to say to us. By failing to relax properly we neglect ourselves. We often ignore the small aches and pains that can be important messages from our body, and this in turn can lead to stress, insomnia and ultimately illness. In this exercise we use a mindfulness technique to give focus to your body and to relax your mind. This technique is best performed lying down and is a good practice to use prior to sleeping:

As I stated above this exercise is best performed lying down, so find a suitable bed or couch to lie on. You may wish to cover yourself with bed clothes or a blanket so that you are warm and comfortable. Lie down on your back with your feet slightly apart and your arms placed by your sides, with your palms facing upwards (palms facing downwards is fine if it is uncomfortable to have them facing upwards). Close your eyes and, as in the first exercise, take three breaths in and out through your nose. As before take twice as long to exhale as it does to inhale and remember to pause at the top of the breath before starting the cycle of exhalation.

Observe the breath coming into your body and your stomach rising as you inhale, and falling as you exhale - notice how you feel. Remember that there is no right or wrong answer to the question of how you feel. Each time you perform the practice you are likely to feel slightly different - the important thing is that you observe and notice.

After your third breath, slowly allow your breaths to form a natural rhythm and to soften as you feel yourself relaxing. It's now time to turn your focus to your body. Start by bringing your attention to your toes – relax your toes and send some of the energy from your in-breath down to your toes. Repeat the exercise by breathing down to your feet, your ankles, your shins and knees. In the same way relax your thighs, your bottom and your lower back. Take your time with the practice and remember to send love and thanks to each part of your body using the energy of your in-breath as you slowly move up your body. If your focus notices an ache or a pain, pause and send healing warmth or healing light from the in-breath to that area of your body.

Give special consideration to your back, shoulders and neck, moving your shoulders up and out to release your heart centre as you relax them. Remember to breathe out any areas of tension that you may find. When you get to your chin, gently swallow to release your tongue and let go of any tension that you may be holding in your jaw. Keep in mind that no part of your body is too small to not merit your attention so consider your cheeks, nose, eyelids, forehead and eyebrows as well as your head as you relax.

Once you have relaxed each part of your body to your satisfaction return your focus to your breathing. You should by now be feeling relaxed and comfortable. Try to feel each in-breath pervade your entire body with warmth, light and energy. Bask in the simplicity of the breath, the moment and the joy of relaxation. Take the time to be grateful for the wonder that is your body before either gently returning yourself to an awakened state or simply allowing yourself to fall fast asleep.

Elements of this exercise come from a technique called Yoga Nidra, which originates from a Hindu tradition.

Most of us experience distracting thoughts spinning around in our heads and for many people this seems to be at its worst at night, particularly when we are stressed or fearful – use this method on a regular basis for relaxation and as an aid to blissful sleep.

NOTES...

CHAPTER 4 – A MEDITATION ON LOVING KINDNESS

Emotion, haste and the noise of the day melt away in meditation. Reconnection allows unconditional love to flow, there is peace and silence. I am loved.

Janice Rooke

This meditation comes from the Buddhist tradition and the original name of this practice in the Pali language is Metta Bhavana. The Pali language is thought to have originated in the Madhesh region of Nepal and is now a 'dead' language rather like Latin – many ancient Buddhist documents are written in Pali. In translation to English, metta means 'love' (in a non-romantic sense), friendliness, or kindness, hence, it translates to 'loving-kindness'. Love or kindness is a positive emotion, something you feel in your heart centre. Bhavana means development or cultivation. By combining the two meanings, the purpose of the meditation is therefore, 'the cultivation of love':

In this practice the meditation is split into five stages of approximately five minutes each. There are meditation applications that can be downloaded to tablets or smart-phones that will time a twenty-five minute meditation and sound (generally chimes or gongs) at five minute intervals so that you can move through the stages, which you may want to make use of. Alternatively, you may wish to take the time that you need for each stage without concerning yourself with the specific length of the meditation.

This exercise is best performed sitting down, either on the floor or in a chair with your feet flat on the floor. It's good to find a place where you are unlikely to be disturbed – somewhere you feel comfortable and secure. Wrapping yourself in a blanket may give you a sense of extra warmth and safety. As always, start the meditation by taking three breaths and then let your breath become shallower as your breath falls into a natural rhythm.

The first stage is about feeling love for yourself. You start by becoming aware of yourself by focussing on feelings of peace, calm, and serenity in your heart area. Observe these feelings and then gently let these sensations grow in strength and confidence. You can imagine an image, like a golden, loving, light flooding your body, or use a phrase such as 'may I be well, may I be happy, may I be free from suffering', which you can repeat in your mind to stimulate the feeling of love for yourself.

In the second stage you think of a good friend. Bring them into your mind as vividly as you can, and think of their good qualities. Feel the link with your friend and your liking for them, and encourage this to grow by repeating 'may they be well, may they be happy, may they be free from suffering' quietly to yourself. You can also imagine a beam of shining light that moves from your heart into theirs.

Please employ the above technique of using a phrase or an image in the next stages of the practice.

In the third stage, think of someone you do not particularly like or dislike — someone for whom your feelings are 'neutral'. This may be someone you do not know well, but someone that you occasionally talk to or see around from time to time. Picture them in your mind, reflect on their humanity, and then include them in your feelings of love and peace.

In the fourth stage think of someone you actually dislike — an enemy. Step back from any feelings of hatred or animosity by thinking of them in a positive way and by sending them love and peace as well.

In the final stage, think of all four people together — yourself, the friend, the neutral person, and the enemy. Quietly contemplate this select group of people before extending your feelings further — send peace and love to everyone around you, to everyone in your neighbourhood; to everyone in your village, your town, your country, and so on throughout the world. Feel waves of loving-kindness spreading from your heart to every person, to all beings everywhere. Enjoy the experience and then gradually relax out of meditation - take three deep breaths and gently bring the practice to an end. Remember to slowly open your eyes only when you have become fully conscious of your surroundings. Ground yourself by drinking a glass of water or other refreshing non-alcoholic drink.

This is meditation is particularly beautiful as it helps us to remember our humanity and it is an antidote to hate. A feature of our emotions is that we can only experience one emotion at a time and the more time that we spend in a positive emotional state the better it is for our health and state of mind. This meditation serves to grow the positive emotions of love and compassion. The more that we practice compassion both in meditation, and in our day to day lives, the more negative emotions such as anger and hate are reduced. Hard as it may be we do need to show compassion towards our enemies as it is necessary for our emotional and spiritual growth. In addition you also need to love yourself - some of our most cruel thoughts and hate we reserve for ourselves. Performing this meditation regularly helps us to forgive both ourselves and our enemies – if everyone performed this simple practice the world would be a better place.

Closing Down

Most of us experience negative energy in our lives. It can affect people in a number of ways and you may notice that there are some people who project negative energy. Such negative energy is both harmful to the person themselves and the people around them. If you are constantly around such people, in either a home or work situation, it can be draining and makes it much more difficult for you to be positive about life. Negative energy can make you feel unhappy even in situations where you previously felt happy. To protect yourself from such situations you may wish to use a closing down technique. The following is a simple 'close down' technique that can be performed after meditation as follows:

To close yourself down simply imagine yourself being enveloped by an orange cloak or bubble that completely surrounds and protects you. Once you have satisfied yourself that you are surrounded with your protective orange cloak, then imagine a blue cloak or bubble that covers the orange cloak. The combination of covering yourself with firstly the orange and then the blue cloak closed you down and you are protected from negativity.

It should be noted that there are many people who believe that closing ourselves down implies that there is something to fear and they suggest that the close down process has the negative effect of also shielding us from beneficial positive energies. Whether or not to use a close down technique is one of personal choice, but it's important to be aware of how to 'close down' your energies so that you can protect yourself from negative energy situations should you wish to. In particular children and adolescents should be taught how to do this as they are especially vulnerable because they are open and easily influenced.

NOTES...

CHAPTER 5 – MANTRA MEDITATION

Cast adrift amongst a billion-billion galaxies, thoughts free of all self-awareness or preoccupation!

Bill Batchelor.

Mantras are often used for meditation and are most commonly associated with Transcendental Meditation. The practice involves the use of a sound or mantra to lead you into a meditative state. In my experience this technique works very well for some people, but others find can find it challenging. In this exercise I have shared with you a Christian method of meditation after John Main OSB (1926-1982). John Main played a major role in the renewal of the contemplative tradition in Christianity. Before John, meditation had become marginalised and had even been described as something that was not part of the Christian tradition. He was able to bring back this ancient tradition of prayer, which is rooted in the Gospels and the early Christian monastic tradition of the desert, though meditation is still unfortunately treated with suspicion in some parts of the Christian church.

Find a place where you are unlikely to be disturbed – somewhere you feel comfortable and secure. Start your meditation as we have before by sitting still, with your back straight, either on the floor or in a chair with your feet flat on the floor. You may consider wrapping yourself in a blanket to give you with some extra warmth and to provide you with a feeling of wellbeing. As always, start the meditation by lightly closing your eyes and taking three deep and long breaths - then let your breath naturally become shallower as it falls into a natural rhythm.

Then, silently begin to recite a single word - a prayer word or mantra - inside your mind. John Main recommended the ancient Aramaic Christian prayer-word 'Maranatha' (translated as 'Come Lord' or 'Our Lord has come') and, as far as I am aware, this is the only mantra used in Christian meditation today – alternatively you can use the universal, 'Om' or another mantra of your choice. If you use 'Maranatha', say it as four equal syllables (ma-ra-na-tha) – you may wish to experiment by sounding one syllable on the in-breath, the next on the out-breath and so on. Keep your breath to the same natural rhythm and give your full attention to the word as you say it. Stay with the same word during the whole meditation and don't visualise, but listen to the word as you say it. Let go of all thoughts (even good thoughts), images and other words. Don't fight or attach yourself to your distractions but let them go by saying your word faithfully, gently and attentively. If you realise that you have stopped saying your mantra or if you find that your focus has wandered simply refocus on your word and start the process again.

As we have discussed previously you can use a meditation timer to time your practice or simply let the meditation come to an end when you naturally feel that it is right. Remember that the instructions that I give you are only a guide and you can experiment within the frameworks given. For example, some people may find music a distraction when performing a mantra meditation, however, others may find it enhances the experience. As always don't forget to ground yourself and, if you feel it's necessary close yourself down.

The joy of this meditation is its simplicity and for some people repeating a mantra is the only way that they can achieve a meditative state. There are many approaches to mantra meditation and in this chapter I have only touched the surface of what is available. I use the Christian example of 'Miranatha' because I wanted to illustrate that meditation is present in all the major religions if you look carefully and also because I find that the multiple syllables of the word help me to meditate.

Resistance to Meditation

I'm mentioning resistance at this time in the course because this is something that all meditation practitioners will experience at some time or another and being aware of it is important - it's often the main barrier to achieving a long-term and successful, meditation practice. Meditation is about training the mind and disciplining your attention. Unfortunately, your attention often doesn't want to be disciplined. Your mind would much rather carry on in its chaotic way, following this thought and that idea as it has done in the past. In summary, unless you are aware of what is happening, your subconscious will always find ways to distract you and find reasons why you are too busy to meditate or why meditation can be put off until tomorrow or another time.

Why we experience subconscious resistance to meditation is not fully clear. Perhaps it's our subconscious fear of the unknown or the unexpected that causes the resistance. What tends to happen is that the resistance is most pronounced just before you are about to make a breakthrough and transform yourself. The subconscious creating a series of reasons why you do not have the time to meditate is generally the main symptom of the resistance. This can result in you missing your meditation sessions and you may eventually stop practicing meditation. Generally, I view resistance as a positive sign that a person is about to make an advancement, but I have witnessed experienced practitioners give up meditation for months and even years due to resistance.

Recognising that you are experiencing resistance to meditation is the best way to overcome it because this awareness allows you to take action against it. One way of doing this is to write out an action plan or schedule that rigorously states when you will meditate. Most importantly you must stick to the schedule and it helps if you make notes in a meditation journal recording how you feel before and after each meditation – by reviewing your notes over a period of time you are likely to notice that you feel better after a meditation than before it. You may also deploy a reward system as a way of motivating yourself to stick to the schedule. For example, you may choose to reward yourself with some meditation music, a crystal or essential oil if you meditate for a week without missing a practice. As I stated previously, resistance tends to occur prior to a breakthrough, hence, patiently sticking to a plan of continued meditation practice will eventually lead away from resistance to a sense of achievement.

Another way of dealing with resistance to meditation is to make the resistance itself the object of your meditation. Examine what feelings are present – for example, anxiety or restlessness? Where are those feelings located? Perhaps you feel them in the pit of the stomach? Is there some tension in the back of the neck? By becoming aware of your emotions and the physical sensations associated with the resistance, you make them the object of your meditation. In summary it then becomes possible to turn your resistance to meditation into another means of meditating and thus, this addresses the challenge of resistance.

NOTES...

CHAPTER 6 – CHAKRA MEDITATION

Meditation for me is going home. Each time I journey home I awaken to the simplicity of Being and I feel instantly relieved. I feel liberated from the stuff that weighs down my physicality and that clouds my mind. When I journey back from my inner space, my reality to the outside world I bring with me my essential Self; I bring with me my inner light. And I feel physically light. I feel at One. Then I can truly live.

MariaElena Cusick

Chakras are centres of spiritual power in the human body. There are many meditations that focus on the areas of your body that are associated with specific chakras. The concepts of chakras feature strongly in the traditions of Hinduism and Buddhism and they are considered to be part of your spiritual rather than your physical body. For the most part meditations focus on correcting over-active or under-active chakras by 'Chakra Balancing', which have the aim of improving your physical and emotional well-being.

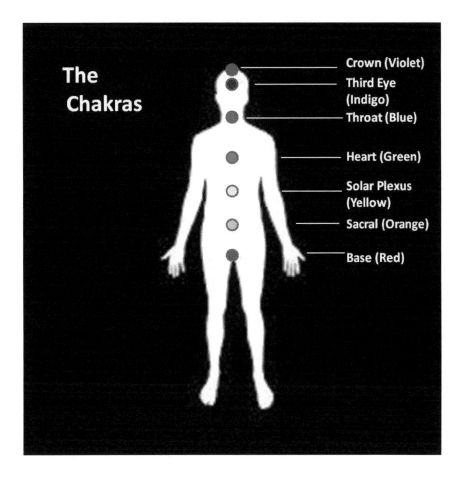

The above diagram shows you the approximate positions of the primary chakras in your body.

There are others, but for this course I only intend to give you a glimpse into the main energy

centres in what Buddhists would describe as your "subtle body". You will notice in the diagram

that each chakra has a different colour and these correspond to the colours of the spectrum.

Some people, whilst meditating on a particular chakra, may notice that that they are able to see

the colour associated with that chakra in their mind or in the area of their body associated with

the chakra. Others do not see any colour, but they do notice a feeling, perhaps warmth or

tingling, in the energy centre that is being focussed on. I mention the above as potential

experiences of a chakra meditation, but don't be concerned if you do not feel or see these things. The most important thing in any meditation is that you observe rather than try to seek any particular outcome.

By meditating regularly, you help keep your chakras functioning smoothly, which in turn promote good physical and mental health, inner peace and creativity, as well as success in your relationships and even the elimination of negative emotions. Whilst hosting a small, weekly, meditation group from my home in Cambridgeshire, England, I've noticed that some people find meditating on certain chakras easier than others, which may be related to chakra blockages. If you research chakra theory you will find the belief that when a chakra's energy becomes "closed" or "blocked", we can develop illnesses and disorders. I have no direct evidence that this is the case; however, I have noticed that people who find it difficult to meditate on a certain chakra show some of the personality traits associated with an imbalance of that particular chakra. It may be that in extreme cases imbalance could lead to illness, but I would caution against any kind of fear response to a chakra imbalance. My belief is that the process of regular meditation will balance the chakras by removing the negative emotions that are a feature of chakra imbalance. To help you be mindful of chakra characteristics I've included a summary description of the primary Chakras with a short review of their features:

The Base or Root Chakra (Red) – Located around the base of your spine. This chakra is all about your stability, grounding, security and survival. If in harmony this chakra gives you control over the world around you and gives you a feeling of being comfortable in your own skin. A balanced Root Chakra will give you a quiet confidence of being able to make things, 'happen'.

The Sacral Chakra (Orange) - This chakra is located approximately one hand's width below your stomach button. The energy here is associated with your emotions - creativity, sensuality, pleasure, sex, and procreation. This energy centre is more about letting go of guilt and frustration and enjoying life, rather than sex. Creative impulses also originate here. Imbalance in this chakra can lead to overindulgence and thrill seeking e.g. extreme sports or activities where we chase an adrenalin rush.

The Solar Plexus Chakra (Yellow) - This chakra is your power base. It is related to willpower, self-esteem and confidence – it is also the centre of your, 'gut feel'. Personal growth also comes from this energy. If this chakra is in balance you will feel in control, but not controlling. Imbalance can lead to a general lack of confidence and you may feel drained by situations and circumstances. People who have an imbalance in this chakra may find it difficult to make decisions. They can be taken advantage of and can give too much of themselves. It's important to be aware that we need to both give and receive energy to live healthily.

Heart Chakra (Green) - Your heart centre. It links your physical and spiritual realms. Many teaching suggest that your heart centre is where your soul lies. It is from here that you derive and grow your capacity for caring, your feelings of self-love, altruism, generosity, kindness and respect. Think here of compassion, forgiveness and hope.

Throat chakra (Blue) - Promotes constructive communication and positive self-expression. Many negative habits are linked to an imbalance in this chakra. They include: gossip, over-eating, smoking and alcoholism.

Third Eye or Brow Chakra (Indigo) – Situated in the centre of your forehead between your eyes. This chakra promotes self-knowledge, wisdom, clairvoyance, insight, and visualization. When balanced, you are highly intuitive, imaginative, and prone to psychic experiences.

Crown Chakra (Violet) - The mystical centre located at the top of your head is the highest of the seven chakras. It is the entrance for, 'Prana' (described in Hinduism as the energy source of all life), into your chakra system. It is from here that you can understand your connectedness with the rest of the universe.

Having balanced chakras is viewed to be highly beneficial to a person's health and wellbeing. The following is a simple exercise that can be used to balance your chakras:

Find a peaceful and quiet room and stand in the middle of it. Turn yourself around by 360 degrees so that you take in the form and dimensions of the room. Carefully adjust your posture so that your feet are approximately a shoulder's width apart and that your head, neck, shoulders and spine are in relaxed alignment. To help you with your posture you may want to imagine yourself being supported by a thin cord attached to the top of your head. As always take three breaths to centre yourself.

Now that you are in a relaxed and upright position partially close your eyes. The next step is to start to extend energy out from your whole body so that it fills the whole room, including the corners. Continue this process for five to ten minutes or until you feel a natural end to the exercise. Observe your body during the practice and notice any feelings or sensations you experience.

Remember to ground yourself, take some deep breaths, bring your awareness back to the room and if you feel it's necessary, close yourself down before fully opening your eyes. Drinking some water or other non-alcoholic refreshment after the exercise is highly recommended. This practice both balances and releases energy from your chakras.

The information that I have provided you with on chakras is a basic overview and there are many, far more detailed, texts and writings, particularly from the Buddhist and Hindu traditions that can provide you with more information should you wish to research further. I personally recommend a book called, 'The Divine Name', by Jonathan Goldman which has an accompanying CD with exercises for the reader to practice. Jonathan approaches chakras from a Jewish traditional perspective and the book teaches techniques for balancing your chakras using a toning or chanting technique. Ultimately it teaches you how to sound what the author believes is the 'Divine Name', which is reputed to have been the name of God given to Abraham on Mount Sinai in addition to the Ten Commandments. In my experience the sounding of the Divine Name has the effect of toning and balancing all of your chakras in a single intonation.

In my view, another form of chakra balancing is 'Reiki', which uses hand-positions that largely focus on the seven major chakras on the body. A Reiki practitioner lays hands on both the front and back of the body and it is used as an increasingly popular form of alternative healing. It is believed to have been developed in 1922 by a Japanese Buddhist called Mikao Usui, but has since been adapted by various teachers across a number of traditions. Today, there are two main branches of Reiki, commonly referred to as Traditional Japanese Reiki and Western Reiki. Reiki primarily uses the Crown, Third Eye and Heart Chakras to channel healing energy through the hands of the Reiki practitioner to the recipient. If you wish to try Reiki, use your intuition to find a practitioner who you trust, and feel comfortable with.

I believe that the simple act of regular meditation in combination with exercising our physical bodies has the effect of balancing our chakras. Becoming more aware of the energy centres in our bodies is very helpful in our spiritual journeys. In this chapter and elsewhere in the course I hope that I can give you some insight into what is a vast topic area. I encourage you to research chakras more fully, but I advise you to avoid any teaching that makes you feel fearful. A key purpose of this course is to present to you a number of different mindfulness and meditation techniques so that you can find practices that work for you. If you find that you struggle with a particular method do not worry about it. Remember that the nature of meditation is that you will find that some sessions are deep and beautiful, whereas at other times you might struggle to stay focused. I encourage you to try different techniques, however, I emphasise the importance of keeping a regular meditation practice over pursuing any specific technique.

NOTES...

CHAPTER 7 - FORGIVENESS

Through meditation I discover the wellspring of renewal, where inspiration is found in the space between each breath and where there is texture to the silence between sounds; a place where I ceases, and experience is.

Helen Dye

Forgiveness is a common concept across many religions and often associated with Christianity, but I find that the purpose of forgiveness is not often well explained. In simple terms, the purpose and lesson of forgiveness is that you only let yourself be hurt by something once. This means that, for your own benefit, you need to quickly let go of negative emotions associated with a person or event that you feel have wronged you in some way. It should be noted that emotional wounds often cause us more pain than those of a physical nature. Forgiveness is a way of healing these mental wounds.

In life there is suffering - people and events hurt us and when they do we need to forgive. If we don't then the fear from what happened in the past gets amplified in our imagination as we replay our hurts again and again in our minds. For most of us this is a common experience – how many times have you replayed an event in your head because you felt that you were mistreated in some way or hadn't handled a situation as well as you would have liked? Such introspection can be harmful and it can be compared to having a splinter in your hand or a thorn in your side that isn't removed. In their extreme such metaphorical thorns can injure and restrict you for the rest of your life.

It is important that we let go any hurt from the past so that our spiritual journey can move forward. Too often people fail to remove their mental thorns, which get buried deeper in their psyches and they find increasingly more sophisticated ways of protecting their thorns from even the lightest touch. Physically we react to even our minor bodily injuries quickly and we all know that removing a physical thorn hurts us more for a short time, but after it is removed, the wound quickly heals and the hurt fades. We are also aware that not removing a splinter or thorn in our body could lead to infection and potentially illness so we take immediate action. In contrast we are less likely to address mental hurts, however, once a mental thorn is removed the inner fear dissipates and we are healed.

We should be mindful that guilt is just fear in another form so it is equally essential that we also forgive ourselves for the hurt that we inflict on others. Mental healing is simply the removal of fear and any act of compassion that we take towards someone else that removes their fear serves to heal them - this healing also has the beneficial effect of being reflected back on ourselves. In simple terms we operated in two modes - we either project fear or we extend love to others, and what we give out we receive back.

Our capacity for forgiveness is profound once it is released. Take for example, the many stories we hear about former prisoners of war becoming firm friends with their former guards and torturers after the conflict, but only after they have both let go of their fear. Keep in mind that when we hurt someone we also hurt ourselves so the tortured and the torturer both need to be healed. This meditation uses the act of forgiveness as a means of removing fear and is therefore a healing process:

As I have suggested in preparation for the previous exercises find a place where you are unlikely to be disturbed – somewhere you feel comfortable and secure. For this meditation it's best not to use a meditation timer, but allow yourself plenty of time (say 30 to 40 minutes) for the meditation so that you won't feel rushed in any way. My observation is that for most people, meditations naturally last for about twenty minutes.

Lighting candles and/or playing some music of your choice can be delightful and add to the ambiance of your situation, but it is not essential. Sit down on a chair with your feet flat on the floor – alternatively you can sit cross-legged on the floor, or on a cushion, if you prefer a more traditional approach to meditation. You may wish to wrap yourself in a blanket if it helps to keep you warm and relaxed. As time goes by you will work out a practice that suits you, but take care not to ritualise your actions – remember that you can always take three breaths in the most hectic of places and shouldn't wait for the quiet peace of your favourite spot to continue your mindfulness exercises.

Close your eyes, keep your back straight and body in an upright position, cup your hands in your lap, with one hand gently laid one on top of the other and relax yourself as much as you can. As always, start the meditation by taking three breaths.

If you have performed the previous exercises, and perhaps started a regular practice, I hope that you are now starting to find it easier to reach a relaxed and meditative state. After your initial deeper three breaths allow your breaths to soften and take on their own rhythm. Continue to be mindful of the breath entering and leaving your body until you feel comfortable and then gently transfer your focus to your heart area. As you breathe in and out through your nose imagine the breath also entering your heart area and similarly, as you breathe out, imagine the breath leaving the centre of your chest.

In many eastern religions the heart area is the seat of the Soul and is generally associated with compassion, empathy, forgiveness and tolerance. Bringing your focus to your heart may allow you to feel some warmth in this area or a feeling of peace or contentment. Without making any judgements observe how your heart area feels and imagine it opening out and expanding to envelope the room. Some people are able to visualise colours – the primary colour associated with the heart is green.

Continue with the exploration of your heart area – remember to observe your feelings without judgement and do not to worry if you don't come across any of the experiences that I've described above – each person is different and has unique experiences of meditation. The important thing is that you are becoming conscious of your inner spirituality and once that awareness starts it will grow.

Let's now commence the process of forgiveness. Whilst keeping your focus on your heart area select an issue that is troubling you. Keep in mind that the purpose of this meditation is to protect you from any further hurt from past situations so remember not to attach yourself to any particular thought or issue – the aim is simply to observe. To start it's generally best to choose a simple issue until you are familiar with the process. For most people the first time subject usually picks itself.

Now allow yourself to focus on the experience that you have been guided towards. As you begin to replay the experience the observation component becomes significant as it will allow you to put some distance between yourself and the person or event that hurt you. It is helpful at this stage to remind yourself of something that you may have forgotten a long time ago - and that is the fact that you are perfect and cannot really be hurt. You are eternal and overflowing with love.

Use this critical piece of information in combination with a focus on your breath to breathe out and let go of any fears or negativity associated with your metaphorical thorn. Take some time to forgive yourself for any actions that you may have taken that could have exacerbated the situation. Observe your concerns fade and lose their importance as you allow yourself to feel protected and to move forward without further hindrance.

Take a few moments to send love and wellbeing to all those that you have forgiven including yourself. Then return your focus to your heart centre and examine how it feels – it should feel a little lighter... a little more joyous.

As with the removal of a physical thorn you may find the removal of mental thorn a little painful, but once it is removed you will feel much better. If the pain becomes intense and you find yourself becoming attached to your thoughts simply revert to following your breath. Observe the cool air entering your nostrils, your stomach and chest rising and the warm air leaving your body as your attachment to your thoughts diminishes.

Let the meditation continue until you reach a natural end and then gently bring yourself back to normality. Remember to ground yourself, and if you feel it's necessary, close yourself down before gently ending your meditation.

You will find that the acts of being grateful and also of forgiveness will increase your levels of day to day happiness. It's likely that you will become more compassionate and gain an ability to look beyond someone's anger or anxiety to the fear that underlies such emotions. This means that we are less likely to react to their fear stimuli and therefore, are able to help them start their process of healing.

You may wish to try this test in your day to day life with someone whom you have a difficult relationship with. Most commonly this may be someone at work such as your boss or a co-worker. The exercise involves sending peace and love to the person that you are having difficulty with. In any meeting or contact that you may have with them focus on your heart centre and consciously send them peace and love – most importantly do not react to any negativity that they may be projecting. If possible try to show that you care and are enjoying their company as much as you can. By consciously taking this approach and looking for the good in the person concerned you will likely find that your relationship with that person improves immensely. I have used this approach many times and people who I previously disliked have become firm friends because I now look at them in a different way – I believe that they have also changed their view of me.

As time goes by you will work out a meditation practices and techniques that suit you, but take care not to ritualise your actions as this can introduce the dogma that is present in many of today's religions – remember that you can always take three breaths in the most hectic of places and shouldn't wait for the quiet peace of your favourite spot to continue your mindfulness exercises. Life is precious and is like gold dust that slowly slips through your fingers so enjoy every minute!

NOTES...

CHAPTER 8 – I AM NOT A BODY

This notion of practice has become central to mindfulness for me; it alleviates the pressure of worrying about the quality or quantity, it liberates me from expectations and simply makes mindfulness a routine which I engage with every day. By treating mindfulness practice as a daily task and not looking for any particular outcome beyond the completion of that task, I have been able to persist with it and paradoxically benefit from it.

Asher Rickayzen

Changing your outlook on your body can have a profound positive impact on your health, both mentally and physically. Accepting firstly that your body is not you and will eventually deteriorate, and then secondly, what and how you think can have a significant impact on the health of your body, is highly advantageous. In considering the latter premise, you may notice that your body often finds it difficult to distinguish between internal and external stimuli. For example, if you dream that you are being chased by a pack of dogs, your heart rate and adrenaline levels will rise in a similar way to a situation where you are actually being chased by a pack of dogs. You may also notice that whether you laugh or whether you cry is determined by the thought process that precedes the bodily process. Similarly if you worry continually about a work situation or a relationship it will have a biological impact on your body. Doctors suggest that that living in a state of stress is very unhelpful to your body and can in itself create illness. It is therefore sensible to conclude that changing the way we think and the attitude that we have towards our daily life can have a highly beneficial effect on the wellbeing of both our mind and body.

The more difficult concept of not thinking of yourself as a body is more challenging. As we grow older we physically decline, our memory isn't as good as it used to be and our thinking isn't quite as sharp as when we were younger. In most of us this creates a fear of growing old. This fear of a physically and mentally deteriorating body is now part of many cultures and people don't like to be reminded of it – as a result old people can be ostracised and become separated from the community that they live in. For some this can lead to great loneliness in old age.

The collective fear of aging that resides in our Western society encourages us to try and look as young as possible and causes us not to value generations older than ourselves. This is different to tribal cultures regarded as primitive, who venerate their old people for their knowledge, wisdom and connection to the spiritual world. For our own happiness we need to reconnect with and value the aged around us. They are simply further down the road of life than we are and we can learn much from their experiences. Treating them with love and compassion is helpful to both you and them. Their bodies may be in decline, but their spirits are eternal and they are on a path that we will surely follow. It is therefore sensible for us to accept the aging process and think about our bodies in a different way.

To use an analogy - it's as though your mind and your body are a car that you bought brand new and then have subsequently driven around in it for a few years and now it's not quite as good as it used to be. To add to your stress you are short of money and this makes you worry because you will never be able to afford to buy another car. Your fear increases with every sign of wear and if a warning light appears on the dashboard it is greeted with panic because it's the only transport that you have.

Let's continue to think about the body as though it was a car - from our previous discussions we know that the body isn't the engine of the car as the body is directed by the mind and the mind generates thoughts, which in turn make the body react – to reemphasise, sad thoughts can cause our body to cry and happy thoughts can make our body smile. Hence, we can consider the mind to be the equivalent of the engine in a car. You will have noticed, if you have performed a number of the meditation exercises in the previous chapters, that you are separate to your thoughts. In meditation we observe our thoughts and try not to become attached to them. We are therefore, not the thoughts – we are the observer of the thoughts. To continue with the car analogy – you are not the car or the engine, you are the driver! This means that at some point in time, when the engine stops, you will open the car door, get out and continue your journey by another means of transport.

To further illustrate the above - from your first childhood memory to the present day you may have noticed that there is a part of you that has remained unchanged. Looking at yourself in the mirror may alert you to the aging of your body, but inside you feel the same. If you ask any older person whether they feel any different inside from when they were young they always respond that they feel exactly the same inside as when they were a child. This supports the view that your body is merely a communication device that allows you to commune with other human beings rather than a body that is actually you. I hope that you will find these analogies comforting, particularly as you get older and your body shows signs of wear and tear:

The exercise in this chapter is simply to ask you not to worry about your body – look after it and treat it with respect, but accept that your body is not you and that, at some point, it will deteriorate and you will not need it anymore. View this meditation with a positive outlook and assume that it will benefit both yourself and those around you. Take three breaths and assume a meditative state as we now have done many times before.

Relax and gently remove any tension from your body and mind as you gently breathe in and out. As you do so imagine that any thoughts that come into your mind are like clouds gently floating across a clear blue sky. Observe each thought without attachment and as you do so recognise that the blue sky that is your mind is bigger than the clouds that are your thoughts. Gently watch each metaphoric cloud disperse into vapour as you sink deeper into your meditation. For a few moments, you may experience a clear mind without any thoughts – a cloudless sky! It's likely that you will only experience this situation for a very small amount of time before thoughts again return. When you become aware again of your thoughts divert your attention to your body. Focus on each part of your body in turn and give thanks. Imagine loving energy entering your body through your heart centre and enveloping your body in healing energy. Send love to any part of your body that you notice tension or have intuitive concern and continue to thank your body for serving you well.

Continue this process until you reach a natural termination, then take three deep breaths,

close yourself down (if you feel that is necessary), wiggle fingers and toes, and then end the

meditation by gently opening your eyes. Remember to ground yourself with a refreshing

glass of water or non-alcoholic drink.

Meditation teaches you to connect with your true self - the eternal, peaceful, part of you and to

differentiate between this and the fearful part of you often referred to as the ego. The ego uses

the body as a source of fear. In this discussion and exercise I am trying to get you to think of

your body in a neutral way, without attachment, and by doing so you remove a primary source

of fear, which in turn will contribute to giving you an improved state of happiness. If you do not

project fear onto your body it will become increasingly healthy. This is because, as we have

discussed, healing is in fact the elimination of fear!

NOTES...

CHAPTER 9 – THE EGO AND YOUR TRUE SELF

Simply sitting quietly, focusing on the breath fills me with a true sense of peace and harmony with my mind and body....

Jeanette Hassall

Through meditation we learn to experience peace. As we carry the practice further we start to realise that our psyche is split into a peaceful mind and a fearful mind. The fearful mind continually distracts us - you may notice that your mind is full of hundreds of thoughts and false imperatives that really have very little meaning. Realising that you are constantly being distracted by thoughts that lead you to valueless attachments is highly beneficial to you on your journey to happiness.

Most people are not aware that they are dominated by a part of themselves that actually wants to do them harm. They frequently let the fearful side of them take control and it immediately separates them from their fellow human beings. This separation leads them to anger, jealousy, attachment to material things, resentment, anxiety and other negative emotions. It is not commonly understood that the more that you love both yourself and those around you the happier you and they become.

By meditating frequently you will become able to connect with the peaceful and loving part of yourself and, as you do so, you will start to more clearly recognise the fearful side of your mind often called the ego. Being conscious of effectively being two people in one body is helpful because it allows us to identify when the negative emotions of the ego are dominant.

Your true self contains the power to create harmony in all relationships and has the kindness to sustain them, whereas your ego will destroy your relationships or at best use them to its own ends. Your true self has a purpose, which is to spread peace and love, whereas your ego is insane, feels constantly under threat and is primarily obsessed with its own survival. A feature of when your ego is in control is the need to constantly strive for something or someone externally that you think will bring you happiness. This is always at some point in the future rather than right now. You should recognise, from previous experience, that even when you achieve your goal, that happiness is always short-lived or elusive and that yet another task has been set for you – there always seems to be one more undertaking to complete before you become truly happy. It's as though you are climbing a mountain where, just as you think you are reaching the summit, you realise that there is still another steep slope to climb. Through meditation and mindfulness practices you will realise that constantly striving for the future or alternatively living in your past are unnecessary and being happy right now is the best goal.

It is worth observing how damaging our egos are to both ourselves and those around us. Our egos are never satisfied and will resort to violence should they not get what they want. Wars have been fought and millions killed just to try to satisfy the insatiable desire of the ego. I have explained that each individual has an ego, but there is also a phenomenon known as the collective ego. The collective ego can be observed most easily at football [soccer] matches where perfectly normal and civilised people can be persuaded to insult and in some circumstances attack supporters of the opposing team merely because they are supporters of the opposing team. This is insane behaviour and yet the daily newspapers provide plentiful evidence that similar behaviours are accepted as part of our daily lives. If you observe court records you will notice, almost without fail, that when a prosecutor in a court of law asks the accused why he committed an act of violence he will almost certainly not be able to adequately explain why. In such circumstances his defence counsel is likely to plead that his client was acting in a manner that was, 'completely out of character'. Interestingly, the same, 'out of character', defence is repeated against many types of crime where the ego has been in control. Clear examples include domestic violence and road rage.

I hope that as you have progressed through this course to this point you have learned a little more about yourself and those around you. The ego and the collective ego both operate by encouraging us to separate individuals or groups of people from our fellow human beings. If we see another person as someone who is not an equivalent of a loved one then we can easily be persuaded that they are different to us. Our egos can then use this perceived difference as a means for fear creation, which in turn makes us feel that we need to protect ourselves. Such defence can quickly turn to hate and attack if we think that a person or persons have the ability to hurt us. As we have discussed above, the ego response can quickly escalate and vary from a minor disagreement to full-blown violence – in the case of the collective ego people can be persuaded to go to war or even commit genocide. The case for relinquishing the ego is therefore, a very strong one.

I was recently listening to a Buddhist nun who was talking to my 14 year-old son while we were visiting a monastery in the Cumbrian Lake District in England. She informed him that every person in the world has one thing in common. He asked what it was. She answered by saying that every person, whether good or bad, wishes to be happy and free from suffering.

I have travelled to many countries in the world and met many different peoples, nationalities and religions – reflecting on the nun's comments I consider her observation to be true. This raises the question, 'If every person in the world ultimately wishes to be happy and free from suffering why are so few individuals in the world actually happy and free from suffering?'

I believe that that the answer to this question lays in the fact that most of us look outwardly rather than within ourselves for our sources of happiness. Even when we have achieved a desired level of material comfort we live in fear that we may at some point lose it and this reduces our level of happiness. In summary, we need to teach ourselves to be happy on the inside so that we can extend love and happiness to those around us on the outside. We do this by using meditation and mindfulness practices to control negative emotions such as anger, hate and jealousy.

The following exercise helps us to become more conscious of when the ego is in control:

Becoming truly peaceful involves relinquishing the ego. The first stage of this process is recognising when the ego is in control of your mind so that you can choose not to follow its direction. It is important to remember that this practice is an undertaking of love rather than an act of aggression against the ego. You are merely becoming mindful of the times when your ego has disturbed your basic happiness. For some people this can be infrequent, whereas for others this can be a very common occurrence.

Enter this practice with a positive feeling that this meditation will benefit both yourself and those around you. As always find a place where you feel comfortable, relaxed and where you are unlikely to be disturbed. Sit in an upright position with your feet flat on the floor, take three breaths and assume a meditative state as we now have done many times before. Relax and gently remove any tension from each part of your body. Let your breath naturally shallow as you breathe in and out through your nose. Take note of how you feel as the air enters and leaves your nostrils. Continue to focus on your breathing for a few minutes before bringing your attention to your heart centre. Imagine your breath also entering and leaving your heart centre as you take air in through your nose. Continue to relax, and as your breath shallows, observe the feeling in your heart area.

As your awareness of your heart centre becomes stronger start to reflect on moments when you have argued or fallen out with someone or where something has annoyed you. Ask yourself why something annoyed you? Did it really matter? If this had been your last day on earth – would you still have behaved in the same way? Would you have let the issue go?

Reflect on the situations where your ego has been bruised and is causing you hurt. Recognise where your ego's hurts go beyond your physical hurts. To help you with this; consider a situation where you have accidentally walked into a chair by accident. The physical pain experienced by the accident will be short lived and quickly forgotten. Compare this to a situation where another person physically hurts you in a similar way. Again the physical pain quickly fades, but how do you feel? For most people the emotional pain of the ego will be felt for far longer than the physical pain. Use this analogy to help you to recognise when your ego is causing you unnecessary pain and let go of your emotional hurts.

Let the inevitable thoughts enter your mind, but try not to follow or attach yourself to them. Where you feel that you may have hurt someone, perhaps recently or at some time in your past, for whatever reason, send them love from your heart centre until your thoughts fade and only silence remains. If someone has hurt you send them forgiveness and love so that they are only able to hurt you once – again the aim is for your thoughts on the matter to become untroubled and fade into insignificance. Try to remember that people are either able to extend love or are in need of love. When someone attacks you they are clearly in need of love and in your meditation use compassion to try to look beyond the attack to see what was troubling them. Can you help them with their hurt?

As you deal with each of thoughts that come into your mind by sending love and forgiveness feel a sense of peace and happiness enter from your heart centre. This feeling of happiness as you let go of your thoughts comes from your true self. If you repeat this practice on a regular basis you will become mindful of the precursors that will lead to your ego taking over and be able take mitigating action. You will progress to a state where you can let harmful emotions be the illusions that they actually are and come to appreciate all forms of life much more than you do today.

Continue with this practice until you naturally reach a point where you feel that the meditation should end. As you return to being conscious of your body and surroundings remember to focus on being grateful for all the people and aspects of your life that make you feel happy. Feel all the smiles, hugs and friendships in your heart centre before you take some deep breaths, wiggle your fingers and toes, and finally slowly opening your eyes to end the meditation. Remember to drink a glass of water after the meditation to ground yourself and, if you feel it is necessary, close yourself down.

It is hard for most of us to accept that we are largely responsible for the reaction that we receive, whether it is love or hate, from the people around us, but I believe this to be true. Your attitude to your fellow human beings has a profound effect on your personal happiness. Becoming more mindful of your reactions to other people, what you say and your own behaviour is a good way to progress. Please use the, 'Three Breaths', exercise from Chapter 1 to help you. Remember that your ego is the first to respond in almost every circumstance. Taking the three breaths allows you to pause and allow your true self time to respond to the situation. You may notice that only one emotion is dominant in your mind at any one time. A small, patient, pause before you speak or take action is likely to be enough to prevent a negative emotion taking hold. When we talked about forgiveness I highlighted that we really only operate in two modes – we either project fear or we extend love.

If we allow the ego to respond first we quickly go down the path of fear projection. When someone shouts at you, your ego's reaction is likely to drive you to want to shout back at them. This in turn can lead to argument, and in its extreme, hate and physical violence. Even when you exit the situation you are likely to find that you are still troubled by guilt, anger and fear. You will have energised your ego and it will be replaying the incident in your head many times over as it tells you that you should have handled the situation in a better way. The ego is rarely satisfied, it will always want more and it will always leave you with a feeling that you are not quite good enough.

In the next 24 hours, make a conscious effort to experience happiness and to extend love in every situation that you find yourself in. Before you enter a shop imagine that you love the person who is going to be behind the counter. When someone appears to be angry try to look beyond the anger. What are they fearful of? How can you help them relinquish their fear? Observe how you feel after the 24 hours?

It is interesting to note that you are never scared when you are helping someone. Please don't take my word for it – witness how you feel when you are helping someone – your ego is left behind. You may also notice that if you are ill and you help someone the symptoms of your disease will not be present for the period when you are actually focussing on helping another person. Many spiritual texts raise the concept of, 'giving in order to receive'. This does not mean giving material things – you may observe that giving materially will usually invoke a feeling of resentment even if you only give the smallest possible amount.

The notion of giving in order to receive means giving love to those around us to receive love and happiness. Giving in this way means that no-one loses and everyone gains. To make this work to its fullest extent we should wish love and happiness to both ourselves and all living things, including our enemies. I wish you well in this practice.

NOTES...

CHAPTER 10 – OBJECT MEDITATION

Sitting in the sun, with a fresh sea breeze, overlooking a tidal creek, with the sound of sea birds. Meditating on a driftwood and being sun bleached, salt dried and wind tossed. Stripped back to our essence, free from who we have become.

Delia Murren.

Object focused meditation is a visual meditation involving an external physical item. We have all experienced object meditations of one kind or another. It's just that we are not always conscious that they are happening. They are the instants when we notice a butterfly, a flower, a waterfall or something else that catches our eye for a few seconds - we forget ourselves, stop thinking about our problems and instead we transcend into a meditative moment where we are being rather than doing. For most people these experiences are fleeting, however, by practising, and becoming more aware of these moments, you can learn to extend them so that that they become 'mini' meditations. As you identify more and more of these opportunities, try to incorporate 10 to 15 of these mini meditations into your day. These small breaks will refresh you and reduce the impact of any stressful situations that you may be experiencing.

One of the advantages of object meditation is that it allows you to meditate with your eyes open. You may find it challenging to meditate with your eyes open initially because you may be distracted by visual stimuli, but it's worth persevering as the benefits of the practice are high. The earlier part of the course will have helped you to deal with distractions and this learning should help you with this technique.

Opening your eyes during a meditation is helpful because the practice can be used from the moment you awake, until you close your eyes to go to sleep. You don't need to meditate in a quiet moment or after you have been working. In fact, you can use this method at any time during the day when you have a few spare moments for yourself. The technique can be used in the middle of the challenges of life because there is no need to wait until you have the right place, the right music and the right lighting – you simply need an object to focus on. It's great to have our perfect meditation spot, but we generally can't run home and meditate when we are presented with an emotional crisis while we are away at work or travelling.

The following exercise will help you to understand the principles of object meditation:

Select an object of your choice to meditate on. The nature of the physical item of your attention is a matter of personal preference and anything from a candle flame to a flower or a piece of driftwood can be used. To illustrate the technique, I'm going to use a red rose as the object of the meditation. Place the rose on a table or a desk so that it's in a position where you can easily focus on it without having to move your head and where it is close enough to you so that you don't have to strain your eyes to see the details of the flower.

Start the meditation by closing your eyes and taking three deep breaths. Once the mind is calm and present gently open your eyes and focus your attention on the rose. Observe every detail of the rose, the colour of the petals, how the light shines on the leaves, the stem and the thorns. Without touching the rose imagine its fragrance and how sharp its thorns are. Notice the contrast between the bright colour of the flower and the green of the stem and leaves. Continue the observation in as imaginative way possible whilst keeping your full attention on the object of your meditation as possible. As your practice progresses, you will find that your thoughts disappear and as a result you start experiencing profound peace and serenity. Slowly watch the rose transform into the object of wonder that it has always been, but perhaps you didn't notice.

As always gently exit the meditation by taking some deep breaths. You can ground yourself by imagining roots growing out from the souls or your feet or root chakra, deep down into the earth, far below your feet. As you end the meditation imagine the roots returning back into your body. This will ground you.

Try the above practice with different objects. You will soon catch yourself deriving intense pleasure from the most mundane of objects.

The above technique can be used to bring peace to a potentially stressful situation by looking for something that can hold your attention. For example, when waiting to board a delayed aircraft at an airport, focus on an item that is around you; there is always a painting, a pot plant, a child playing or something in the architecture that can draw your attention. It is noticeable that when you bring such focus to bear on the object your stress levels drop and you start to feel calm and contented. The following is another practice that uses an internal object to focus your attention:

It is also possible to use the object meditation technique to a make something internal an object of meditation. For example a pain or a hurt can be used. If you have a pain in your leg you can make it an object of your meditation. The technique is to focus your attention onto the pain in the same way as you would an external object. Observe your pain, what does it feel like – is it hot? Is it focussed on a single point or does it move around the area of your hurt? Is there a texture to your pain? Is it continuous or does the intensity vary?

Once you start to observe and understand your pain you can start to breathe healing energy to it. Imagine a healing light or healing warmth surrounding your injury - with every out breath let a little of the pain dissipate away. Experiment with the technique to see if you can successfully heal headaches, other aches, pains and, most importantly, emotional hurts by making them an object of your meditations.

NOTES...

CHAPTER 11 - YOUR PURPOSE

Mindfulness is in direct contradiction to the everyday abstraction of things. What is astonishing about meditation is that such a simple technique can promote an immediate return to mindfulness and to its physical benefits. Mindfulness, in this sense at least, is an effective attempt to return to the fullness of being.

Kevin Rhowbotham

As we near the completion of the course I thought that it would be helpful to summarise the elements of discussion and learning from the previous pages. This short-course starts with the very simple exercise of taking three breaths. From this uncomplicated start we have examined a number of meditative techniques that included relaxation practices, mantra and chakra meditations along with mindfulness techniques that demonstrate the benefits of forgiving and being grateful. I have suggested that your body is not you and is merely a communication device that allows you to connect with your fellow human beings. In addition, I have talked about the dangers of allowing your ego to become dominant and discussed the negative impact of the 'collective' ego on the world as we know it.

A key message from the course material is the importance of connecting with your 'true self'. By using the meditation and mindfulness practices described in this document you will start to break down any barriers that you may have with those around you. I hope that you will come to realise that there are no real differences between yourself and your fellow human beings. It's helpful to understand that individuals, who we regard as criminals, are merely people who have put the thoughts of their egos into physical action. For the most part we think of lawbreakers as being totally different from ourselves, but is this really the case? How often have our own thoughts been less than pure? Perhaps in the pressurised moment something stayed our ego's hand, but most of us have experienced times when negative emotions could have caused the fragile nature of our civilised life to disintegrate. As Jesus said, 'Let he who is without sin cast the first stone'.

The truth is that we all need love, and when you are in need of love, you are likely to behave in a way that usually hurts both yourself and those around you. Conversely through meditation, mindfulness and the connection with your true self you will be able to reach a position where you are able to both love yourself and other people. It is important to note that you must first love yourself before you can extend love to others. Despite our tendency to hurt other living creatures, often we reserve the worst punishment, and the worst torture, for ourselves. When you feel that you have done something wrong it is vitally important that you learn to forgive yourself for what you perceive are your misdemeanours – the exercise in Chapter 7 will help you with this.

Without the constant connection with the loving energy of the universe you run the risk of spreading yourself too thin and in such circumstances love can turn to resentment as you feel that other people are taking too much of your time and energy. It is therefore essential that you make time for both yourself as well as those around you. Initiating a daily meditation practice is a way of doing this, but it's best to be relaxed rather than 'religious' about this. How many people feel guilty because they haven't attended a church, a mosque or a synagogue as frequently as they feel they should? Remember that guilt is another form of fear and the purpose of this course is the elimination of fear. Try to make your meditation sessions a source of pleasure and something that you look forward to. Each time that you meditate a little bit of fear leaves you and a little more love enters your heart. When circumstances prevent you from a formal meditation you can always 'take three breaths' or perform an object meditation to centre yourself before continuing with the opportunities in life. Remember that you are likely to experience resistance to meditation just before you make a breakthrough, so perseverance with a daily practice, in all its forms, is worthwhile.

When you are faced with one of life's challenges try to look at it as an opportunity rather than something to fear. Life can be full of things that we don't particularly like and we spend a lot of our time trying to avoid situations and people that we dislike. Changing your attitude to the situations and people that you avoid may actually be what life is about. Those of us who are parents will know that our children rarely want to do the things that we know are going to be good for them when it is first presented to them. I think that most of us remember the trauma of learning to ride a bicycle, however, we now only carry the joy and extra freedom that cycling gave to us when we were children.

In your life you are continually presented with many options and it can be difficult to decide, which choice is best for you. It is interesting to note that in life similar situations will present themselves to you again and again. Have you noticed that, despite your avoidance efforts, situations continually occur where you are forced to spend time in places or with people that you are actively trying to avoid? It's as though something is giving you another opportunity to correct what went wrong previously. You've been picked up, brushed down, sat back on the seat of your bicycle, kissed on the forehead and asked to ride, so that you can experience something joyous.

A friend of mine was asked on three separate occasions and by three separate Reiki Masters if she wanted to learn Reiki. She asked me if I thought that she should take up the offer. When I asked her if the training would be expensive, she replied that each master had offered to train her for free. I then asked how many Reiki Masters she had previously met. She confessed that up until that time she had not been aware of meeting any Reiki Masters before and had only recently realised Reiki was a form of healing. With much laughter we agreed that perhaps she was being guided to learning Reiki. She has since been Reiki attuned and with much happiness, practices it on her friends and family.

Consider an oak tree in the middle of a field, its leaves and branches moving gently in the breeze. Every summer it grows acorns in an attempt to reproduce, in the autumn it drops its leaves, becomes dormant and another year is marked by a ring in its trunk. This cycle of living and procreation appears to be the tree's purpose and yet, the oak also has an unconscious purpose in the world - in combination with its plant relatives it creates much of the Earth's oxygen from the carbon dioxide that it absorbs as part of its photosynthesis process. This in turn allows other organisms, such as human beings, to flourish and prosper.

If you reflect on nature in general you will observe that every animal and plant, from the plankton to the eagle, operates in equilibrium with each other. Man is probably the only organism that has any real awareness that this equilibrium exists. Perhaps the question that we should ask ourselves is, 'Does man have an unconscious purpose in the world?' Religious and spiritual teaching suggests that there is more to us than our daily lives of eating, sleeping, daily chores and pleasures.

Often we forget how miraculous our world actually is. Without thinking we change the equilibrium – we cut down rain forests, favour certain animals with our breeding programmes and release greenhouse gases into the atmosphere as a by-product of our unconscious desire to separate ourselves from nature. Our wish to create is unstoppable, but, for the most part, it is not a loving creation – it is the creation of the ego. Too often we destroy in order to construct and we replace the natural world with something far less sophisticated in comparison. The nomadic civilisations that for centuries lived in harmony with the land have all but been wiped out and perhaps much has been lost because we just simply did not let them teach us anything.

The universe is something that most of us don't want to think about in any meaningful way because it really hurts our minds to do so. We clearly grasp that we are sitting on a rather large rock that is orbiting around an even larger sun, in a vast universe. Physicists propose that the universe is constantly expanding and that it all started from a point of singularity known as the big bang. They even suggest that there parallel dimensions with multiple universes. Trying to grasp the concept of infinite universe after universe and parallel dimensions is really taxing and it's thinking that most of us avoid. Against this scientific back drop there is a spiritual dimension, which also suffers from a multiplicity of opinion and often relies on belief rather than tested experience. Taking a broad view of scientific and religious opinion tends to leave us both uncertain and confused. How amongst all this uncertainty and confusion do you find a spiritual purpose in life?

I discussed the difference between your ego and your true self in Chapter 9. At the beginning of the course I stated that the purpose of this curriculum is the elimination of fear. I must emphasise that being guided by your ego is a route to fear. Meditation is primarily the way to connect with your true self and mindfulness is the way to remain connected during our daily lives. Being aware of how you feel from moment to moment allows you to adjust your attitude, actions and behaviour away from the direction of your ego. Feeling fearful is a sign that your ego is in control. A practical way of reconnecting you with your true self, in such circumstances, is to 'take three breaths'. At other times you may need to take a longer meditation or join a group meditation to centre yourself. As you continue a meditation practice you will notice that your recovery time will improve and that the periods where you feel anger, guilt, anxiety, etc. will reduce. Enlightenment is a journey and sometimes we take the long, winding road rather than the direct route.

My above statements strongly suggest that finding certainty in an ever changing universe is hard because there are so many things that we don't understand. Uncertainty is something that we must accept in our spiritual journeys and within this framework of uncertainty; we should look for the things that make us happy in our heart centres to guide us. In summary we should look for inner happiness and this will lead us to our true purpose. I emphasise that 'drifting' without any purpose is not a good option. A boat that is set out to drift without anyone to man the tiller is unlikely to reach a desired destination. Be guided by your heart centre, let go of past hurts and avoid any actions that may harm other people or force you to strive for happiness tomorrow because they will be, almost certainly, ego driven.

The final meditation is aimed at guiding you to your purpose in life:

This final meditation has been split into parts, which I would like you to perform over three consecutive days. The idea is that the results from the first meditation will help you with the second and then subsequently, the third. If you find a particular meditation difficult you may wish to repeat a day and then continue with the next meditation so that the practice takes four or five days or perhaps longer. Each meditation focuses on a specific area with the aim of removing any blockages that may prevent you from achieving enlightenment or slow your journey.

For each practice I would like you to take the following preparation steps:

As you have now done many times before, go to the place where you regularly meditate, sit down on your favourite chair or cushion and assume a relaxed, upright, meditative pose, with your feet flat on the floor. Commence your meditation with the attitude that it will benefit both yourself and those around you. Close your eyes, take three breaths, and relax into a meditative state. Make sure that every part of your body is relaxed and that you send love and warmth to any aches and pains that you may have.

Day 1

Take some time to complete the initiation exercise, making sure that you have fully conversed with your body and then return your attention to your breathing. To eliminate any fear that may be associated with your body remind yourself that you are a spirit, not a body, and that you are free – repeat in your mind three times, 'I am a spirit, not a body and I am free'.

Use the above mantra to expand your conscious so that your energy swells beyond your body and fills the room or the space around you. Feel all your self-imposed restrictions melt away as you experience the freedom that this brings. Reach out to the trees, the land, the sky, the oceans and all living creatures and recognise your oneness with each of them.

Before you start the process of gently exiting your meditation remember to give thanks in a way that assumes that you are now fully connected with the oneness of all things.

To end the meditation take three deep breaths, bring your focus back to the room whilst wiggling your fingers and toes before gently opening your eyes. You may find it refreshing and helpful to drink a glass of fresh, clear, bright water as a way of grounding yourself and to fully end your practice.

Over the next 24 hours frequently, 'take three breaths' and use the mantra, 'I am a spirit, not a body and I am free', to centre yourself and remind you of the meditation.

Day 2

Complete the preparation steps as they are described above and allow yourself to enter a deep meditative state. From this place of complete freedom send love to yourself, your family and your friends, those you have neutral feelings about and finally your enemies in equal measure. Take a little time to overlook any grievances that may exist between yourself and those around you.

You may find that there are people in your life that you find it hard to forgive or events that you find it challenging to overlook. If this happens it is important that you don't attach yourself to the thoughts that are preventing you from forgiving. Simply observe and remember that you should not allow yourself to be hurt both by the physical person or event and then by the thoughts in your head. Let go of these thoughts and do not let experiences of the past hold you back on your journey. If this is difficult you can repeat this exercise over another twenty four hours or move on to the next meditation and return to this stage to see if the later practice helps you to deal with your challenges of forgiveness.

As in Day 1, before you start the process of gently exiting your meditation remember to give thanks in a way that assumes that you are now fully connected with the oneness of all things.

To end the meditation take three deep breaths, bring your focus back to the room whilst wiggling your fingers and toes before gently opening your eyes. As on the previous day you may find it refreshing and helpful to drink a glass of fresh, clear, bright water as a way of grounding yourself and to fully end your practice.

During the next twenty four hours, prior to the next meditation, continue to focus your attention on being grateful and try to be mindful of what is happening right now rather than what might happen next or what you may have experienced previously. If you find yourself daydreaming, take three breaths and then bring yourself back to the present moment.

Day 3

Complete the preparation steps as they are described above and allow yourself to enter a deep meditative state. Bring your focus to your heart centre. As you do so start to review your day and try to remember the things that made you happy. Focus on being grateful for even the smallest thing that contributed to your inner well-being during the last twenty four hours and give thanks.

As you experience this spiritual freedom continue the exercise of being grateful by widening your examination from just today to the parts of your life that make you feel truly happy in a broader sense. What activities make you happy and are truly effortless to you? When you perform these activities how does it make the people around you feel? Are they happy along with you or is your joy dependent on their relative unhappiness when compared to you? This is important as true happiness cannot be found where there are winners and losers.

Reflect on the areas of your life that make you enthusiastic, happy, peaceful and joyous. Can you spend more of your time in these areas? Would your life be enhanced if you improved your relationship with those around you? Are there specific individuals that you need to love and forgive so that your relationship with them doesn't slow your journey?

As you gently ask yourself these questions remember to step back from any emotional response that you may have, focus on your heart area and observe your personal challenges as though you are viewing those of an another individual who you have no particular attachment to.

There is no need to worry or expect an immediate response – simply relax, enjoy the experience and ask for help with any problems that you may have that could lead you away from true happiness. Have faith and assume that the answers will come to you and your concerns will be resolved for you.

Before you start the process of gently exiting your meditation remember to give thanks in a way that assumes that you have already been granted the happiness that you have been requesting.

To end the meditation take three deep breaths, bring your focus back to the room whilst wiggling your fingers and toes before gently opening your eyes. To fully end your meditation ground yourself with water or a cleansing tea.

In the following days be mindful of how you feel and pay particular attention to any feelings that you may have in your chakras. If you feel that you want to repeat any of the above meditations then do so as this will help you remove any blockages that you may have. Continue to observe, forgive and feel grateful for those around you. Feel confident that your challenges are being resolved and try to squeeze every little piece of enjoyment that you can out of each day by living in the present. Wherever you are try to feel the connection between the Earth and the soles of your feet. When you eat your breakfast focus on the miracle that is the bread in your hand – it has taken billions of years of universal evolution to reach you. Feel happy as you sip every delicious mouthful of tea and be at peace. Remember that you yourself are a miracle, smile and go out and extend love for every moment of your day.

This meditation contains elements of prayer in it. Prayer is an often misunderstood phenomenon. Many people are very cynical about prayer; primarily this is because, for most of us, prayer does not appear to work. In the above meditation you are connecting with you true self and then asking for guidance. It is important to understand how the universal mind or whatever you wish to call the divine actually works.

I have discussed the ego and the true self and explained that, at any one time, one or the other is in control. When the ego is in control it's rather like a small child who demands of an adult to be allowed to perform a task that is way beyond his ability. Knowing that the child's will is very strong, and that he needs to learn, the grownup allows the child to attempt to perform the task. The adult watches as the child begins the activity and sighs as things quickly go wrong. For most children there is only a short period before he asks the adult for help. As soon as the request for help is received the adult steps in and helps the child. The grownup and the child then work on the undertaking together and the task is quickly completed to the satisfaction of all. Sometimes a particularly wilful child will refuse to ask for help and he or she gets increasingly frustrated when they can't perform the activity on their own. Eventually, unable to complete the task, the child throws a tantrum, blames the adult and storms off in tears of unhappiness.

Unfortunately, most of us live our lives like the wilful child in the above simile – we are either reluctant to or ignorant of how to ask for help. Prayer is a way of asking for help. There are two elements to prayer that you should consider at this point. Firstly you need to have a willingness to ask for help and secondly you need to have an absence of fear. Your life has been dominated by your ego and, as we have discussed, this is akin to the small child refusing to be helped by its father or mother. Once you realise that living according to your ego makes you fearful you can, through meditation and mindfulness, change your attitude and relinquish your fears by simply asking for help and guidance – test this by asking for help from your true self with anything that is worrying you. By allowing yourself to be guided by your true self you will come to realise that you are not alone. This guidance will ultimately give you both direction and happiness in life, but you may be surprised by how subtlety this happens. It's unlikely that there will be a revolutionary event as revolutions tend to be the work of the ego. What you will find is that you will experience small changes in your attitude to the things and people around you. As your attitude changes your life will start to fall into place and cease to be a continuous effort. In particular you will be more aware of the world. You may feel that you have been awakened to life after years of ignorance.

A sign that a change has occurred within you is that people will come to you for help. When they do you will wonder how to help them and what to do. My advice is to remember that pupil and teacher are equal and that you will gain as much from the association as the person who is asking for help. You may wish to start your relationship with them by teaching them to take three breaths.

NOTES...

FURTHER READING

I guide you to the following texts that you may find helpful to read alongside your meditation

practice. Some books are easier to read than others – I've selected them to give you a broad

overview of meditation from differing perspectives. Some of the reading is very practical,

whereas other material is quite esoteric and theoretical. I leave you to make your own

opinions:

40 Mudras - start by number five

Aurelia Fellini (Author), Sascha Fröhlich (Author)

The healing energy of the mudras. Mudras are symbolic hand and finger gestures that are used to worship the gods, to communicate and as a medium of expression in the Indian dance. These hand gestures and their effects have been popular in our society for quite some time. In Yoga and in meditation mudras are used on a regular basis.

In this book you will learn how to effectively use the 40 most important yoga hand gestures and what their effect is. In text and in picture, these mudras are easy to comprehend and easy to learn for anyone. Ideas, tips and tricks are helping you to successfully perform these mudras.

This book is suitable for beginners, as well as advanced learners. The practical exercises can be used whenever, wherever and are easy to become part of your everyday routine. This book is a good reference to look-up individual exercises.

Publisher: Bookrix (26 Jun. 2014)
ASIN: B00SLUW0KE

A Course in Miracles

A Course in Miracles "The only edition that contains in one place all of the writings that Dr. Helen Schucman, its Scribe, authorized to be printed"

Publisher: Foundation for Inner Peace; 3rd edition (21 May 2008)
Language: English
ISBN-10: 1883360269
ISBN-13: 978-1883360269

A New Earth: Create a Better Life

Eckhart Tolle's A New Earth will be a cornerstone for personal spirituality and self-improvement for years to come, leading readers to a new levels of consciousness and inner peace.
By Eckhart Tolle

Publisher: Penguin (1 Jan. 2009)
Sold by: Amazon Media EU S.à r.l.
Language: English
ASIN: B002RI97IY

Chakra Balancing

by Davina DeSilver

A quick and easy read, packed with down to earth tips and ideas you can use to start balancing your chakras and working with your energy system right away. This particular book is to help those relatively new to the chakras get a better understanding of them. It gives practical ways to start balancing and without too much effort you'll be talking the language of energy. You'll discover the signs of a healthy functioning chakra, as well as signs of imbalance and ways to bring balance back to each chakra.

Publisher: CreateSpace Independent Publishing Platform (16 April 2013)
Language: English
ISBN-10: 1482599651
ISBN-13: 978-1482599657

Teach Only Love: The Twelve Principles of Attitudinal Healing

by Gerald G. Jampolsky

Dr. Jampolsky believes there is another way of looking at life that makes it possible for us to walk through this world in love, at peace and without fear. This other way requires no external battles, but only that we heal ourselves. It is a process he calls "attitudinal healing," because it is an internal and primarily mental process. Jampolsky believes that attitudinal healing, when properly practiced, will allow anyone, regardless of her circumstances, to begin experiencing the joy and harmony that each moment holds, and to start her journey on a path of love and hope.

Publisher: Atria Books/Beyond Words; New Expanded edition (4 Oct. 2011)
Language: English
ASIN: B005OK5KNI

The Divine Name: Invoke the Sacred Sound That Can Heal and Transform

by Jonathan Goldman

What if there was a technique for sounding the personal name of God that could change the world?

Publisher: Hay House UK (15 Sept. 2015)
Language: English
ISBN-10: 140194888X
ISBN-13: 978-1401948887

ABOUT THE AUTHOR

M. A. Worthington-Hassall came across meditation following a request by a friend to attend a meditation session in a village near his home in Cambridgeshire. Being a scientist and somewhat of a cynic he almost didn't attend the meeting, however, out of politeness, he turned up at the session. He took part in three meditations over a period of approximately ninety minutes. On the third meditation he transcended in some way. The result of this transcendence changed his life and has resulted in years of meditation, his qualification as a meditation teacher and this short course.

The author was born in Manchester and raised in Cheshire, England. His career started at Rolls Royce Motors Limited in Crewe where he served an apprenticeship. After completing his apprenticeship and extensive travel in 1980's Africa, he took up a degree course at Imperial College, University of London. He studied Geology at Imperial and later became a Master of Science (MSc) in Sedimentology following further study at Birkbeck College. On leaving university he joined the oil industry and then moved into banking and insurance in the City of London where he is currently a Chief Risk Officer, Non-Executive Director and a specialist in emerging markets. He continues to travel extensively across the world both with his work and with his family.

M. A. Worthington-Hassall is married with two children and lives in the rural county of Cambridgeshire, England.

Made in the USA
Columbia, SC
14 May 2017